Pocket Book of
Dragons

First published in 2025
by Riverside Press, an imprint of
UniPress Books Ltd
World's End Studios
London SW10 0RJ
United Kingdom

Copyright in the Work © UniPress Books Ltd 2025

ISBN 978-1-917226-11-0
ISBN (ebook) 978-1-917226-12-7

All rights reserved. No part of this book may be reproduced, stored in a retrieval system or transmitted in any form or by any means, without prior permission in writing from the publishers.

Publisher: Jenny Manstead
Associate publisher: Daniel Mills
Commissioning editor: Jason Hook
Project manager: Ruth Patrick
Designer: Luke Herriott
Copy editor: Blanche Craig
Picture researcher: Stephen Behan

Printed in China

riversidepress.co.uk

Page 4: Sumptuous Gothic treatment of the St George legend, by 15th-century Catalan master Bernat Martorell.

Pocket Book of
Dragons

MYTH, MAGIC & MEANING

JOEL LEVY

RIVERSIDEPRESS

Contents

Introduction 6

Chapter I
Ancient Dragons 12

Chapter II
Eastern Dragons 32

Chapter III
Wyrms 52

Chapter IV
Christian Dragons 74

Chapter V
Dragons of Fable and Folklore 96

Chapter VI
Literary Dragons 116

Chapter VII
Dragon Hunting 136

Further Reading 156
Index 158
Credits 160

Introduction

~

'A dragon is no idle fancy. Whatever may be his origins, in fact or invention, the dragon in legend is a potent creation of men's imagination, richer in significance than his barrow is in gold.'

J. R. R. Tolkien, 'Beowulf: The Monsters and the Critics' (1936)

In cultures around the world and throughout history, the dragon figures as the prototypical and ultimate monster, the mythical beast to rule them all. In 2013 a scientific study attempted to trace the origins of the dragon archetype using the tools of phylogenetic analysis, a technique in which genes (or in this case, memes or story elements) from dispersed modern populations are compared, to work out where and when they came from. The study concluded that the foundational attributes of the dragon myth or concept originated at least 75,000–100,000 years ago, in southern Africa, amongst humans who went on to spread it across the globe, either through migration or cultural transmission. This study is not

Opposite: Lancelot battles a dragon, in an illustration from a 14th-century manuscript of Arthurian romance.

Introduction

widely accepted, and as this book explains, attempting to pin down a single origin for such a protean monster is likely to be a hopeless quest.

Yet while their origins, attributes and symbolism may vary, dragons remain recognisable whether in ancient Mesopotamia, medieval Europe or modern China. This rich and diverse history has stored up for the contemporary reader an unparalleled hoard of fabulous treasure – fabulous in the true sense of the word, for this is a trove of myth, legend, folklore and fiction. Iconic in word and image, the dragon enthrals and entertains, spinning its glamour of enchantment for us today as it did for heroes from Marduk to Sigurd, Beowulf to Bilbo. This *Pocket Book* encompasses multitudes, telling thrilling tales of adventure and peril from ancient epics such as the *Enuma elish* of Babylon to modern-day classics including *The Hobbit* – explaining the symbolism and meaning of the dragon in art, religion and folklore, probing the origins of the myths and the real-world inspirations behind them, and detailing the extraordinary diversity of dragons in stories and fables from around the world.

Following a historical and cultural arc from the ancient roots of myth and literature to their modern incarnations, the *Pocket Book of Dragons* explores dragons in ancient Mesopotamian and Greek myths, including Tiamat and the Hydra, and describes the complex and sophisticated dragon traditions of Asia. The distinctive wyrms of Norse and Celtic myth and legend lead to a consideration of the archetypal dragon-slayers, Sigurd and Beowulf, soon to be supplanted by the Christian heroes for whom the dragon was the symbol of evil. Medieval European folk tales offer a rich panoply of dragon types and stories, feeding into the development of the Western literary tradition of dragons, so important in the development of the fantasy genre. Special features delve into the caverns of dragon lore, examining the iconography of dragons in heraldry and art, the natural biomechanical constraints that make the dragon an impossible fable, the classic attributes and habitats of the dragon, the extraordinary cultural range of the dragon archetype and the latter-day proliferation of dragons in the media. Dragons have spawned a wonderful breadth of artistic and cultural depictions, ranging from the ancient friezes of the Ishtar Gate to the elaborate illuminations of medieval bestiaries, and from the intricate coils of Japanese netsuke to the fantasies of Leonardo da Vinci. The *Pocket Book of Dragons* draws on these and many other sources to depict dragons in all their wonder, ferocity and glory.

Overleaf: A 14th-century tapestry depicting Satanic evil as a seven-headed dragon, in a scene from the Apocalypse of St John.

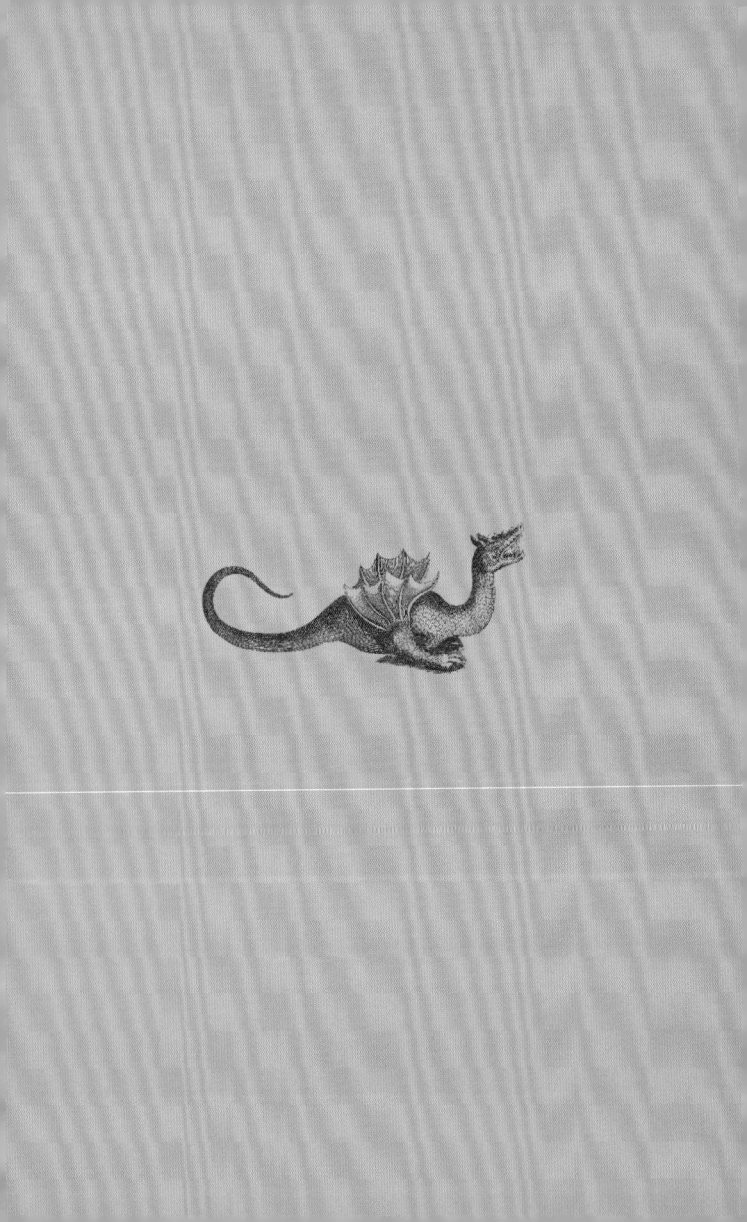

Chapter I

Ancient Dragons

Dragons of the
Ancient World

Chapter I

Dragons appear in some of the earliest recorded literature, and there is some evidence from prehistory that the concept was already potent. The carvings at Turkish site Göbekli Tepe, which predate the first Mesopotamian civilisations and the start of history, show recognisable serpent-dragon figures. So by the time that the dragon featured in the epics of ancient Babylon, India and Greece, it was probably already a culturally embedded archetype.

These ancient dragons were often very different from the modern, Western conception of such creatures, which is the result of a long evolution in form and character that the rest of this book will trace. They rarely had wings or legs, and were not generally associated with treasure (although the Colchian dragon, who guarded the Golden Fleece, was an obvious exception). In most cases they were much closer to snakes, and use of the term dragon in contexts such as the legends of ancient Babylon and Greece should generally be understood to refer to a serpent-dragon, differentiated from everyday snakes by virtue of size, ferocity, malevolence and special powers, typically related to poison, storms and great winds.

In creation myths, such as those of Mesopotamia and India, these serpent-dragons represent chaos, which must be overcome to establish the ordered world in which humans can flourish. In other words they are chthonic entities, linked to the most ancient, even pre-human aspects of cosmology, making them powerful, threatening and strange.

Ancient Dragons

Above: *Jason and the Dragon* by Salvator Rosa *c.*1663.

Chapter I

Ancient Mesopotamian Dragons

~

In the *Enuma elish*, the creation epic of Babylon, the primal goddess of the oceans, Tiamat, is a great dragon whose congress helps to create the gods and whose destruction by the hero Marduk gives rise to the heaven and earth. In form, Tiamat is represented as a hybrid monster with leonine front legs, a giant serpentine body and a horned head. She is just one incarnation of the long tradition of dragons in ancient Mesopotamian myth, in which the (often female) dragon represents chaos and must be overcome by the (usually male) hero who represents order. Tiamat probably helped inspire Christian conceptions of Satan and the form taken by monstrous evil.

The tradition of serpent-dragons can be traced from Tiamat back through earlier versions such as Labbu, 'the Raging One', a great marine serpent monster that, according to a tablet from the Library of Ashurbanipal, was specifically designed by the god Enlil to punish errant humans, but which ran amok, lashing his colossal tail and breathing out storms. Labbu in turn was preceded by the serpent-god Ninazu, possibly the oldest Mesopotamian god of the underworld, who was closely associated with snakes, and particularly with the *mušhuššu*, a dragon-like

Above: Marduk pursues a chaos monster, possibly Tiamat, in a drawing of a bas relief from 7th-century-BCE Nineveh.

mythological creature from Mesopotamian myth and iconography, most famously adorning the Ishtar Gates of ancient Babylon. *Mušhuššu* (pronounced 'moosh-hoosh-shoo') means 'furious snake'; it was a hybrid combining the head and scales of a snake, the legs of a lion, the claws of an eagle and sometimes the tail of a scorpion.

Intriguingly, the *mušhuššu* resembles descriptions of the *mokele-mbembe*, a supposed living dinosaur reported by natives of the Likouala swamplands of the Congo in west Central Africa, and has been sought after ever since by cryptozoologists. One wild theory is that in ancient times, a specimen was taken to Babylon, so that the *mušhuššu* was modelled on a real animal.

Chapter I

The Greek *Drakōn*

~

The word dragon derives from the ancient Greek *drakōn*, denoting a serpentine monster similar to a snake, but with added threat and power. Dragons in Greek myth and legend were often associated with water and caverns, and typically spat or breathed poison, although some were associated with fire.

In Greek myth dragons proliferate. The chthonic world serpent Python (similar to Jörmungandr, the world serpent of Norse myth) parallels its more ancient counterparts, and also perishes at the hands of a heroic god-hero (in this case, Apollo). But there are other varieties too: the Lernaean Hydra, which did battle with Hercules, who also fought the similarly many-headed Hesperian dragon Ladon; the Colchian serpent, which guarded the Golden Fleece until dispatched by Jason (or possibly Medea). Medea had her own dragons; serpentine monsters that drew her flying chariot. Troy and Ethiopia were plagued by *cetae* (dragon-like sea monsters), destroyed by Hercules and Perseus respectively.

An entire city-state, Thebes, claimed descent from a serpent-monster, the Ismenian dragon, described by Ovid as having 'a wonderful golden crest; fire flashed from its eyes, its body was all puffed up with poison, and

Ancient Dragons

Above: Athena rescues Jason from the jaws of the Colchian dragon, on a 5th-century-BCE kylix.

Overleaf: Carle Van Loo's *Perseus and Andromeda*, c.1737, shows a *ceta* with mammalian characteristics.

from its mouth, set with a triple row of teeth, flickered a three-forked tongue'. The hero Cadmus killed it with an iron javelin, and Athena instructed him to sow the ground with its teeth, whereupon there sprang up an army of warriors who battled until only five remained; these became the founding fathers of Thebes.

Chapter I

Vritra the Serpent-Dragon

~

Perhaps the oldest written account of a battle between dragon and dragonslayer is preserved in the ancient Sanskrit hymns of the Rig Veda, composed in South Asia between 1500 and 1200 BCE. Verses tell of the epic showdown between Indra, king of the gods, and the great serpent-dragon Vritra, 'the enveloper' or 'the storm cloud'. Vritra was one of the asuras, the dark gods of Hindu cosmology, roughly equivalent to demons. He was also known as Ahi, the snake.

Originally created when the magic plant/elixir of the gods, soma, was cast into fire, Vritra was said to have grown to monstrous size (an arrowshot in all directions). Eventually he became so vast that he held back the primordial waters and enveloped the universe, hence his name. There are obvious parallels with the world serpent of Norse myth (see page 57), and more particularly with the myth of Marduk and Tiamat (see page 16). As in the Babylonian myth, a divine hero had to slay the dragon-serpent of chaos to bring order to creation.

In the case of Vritra, the Rig Veda describes Indra, fuelled by soma and wielding thunderbolts, slaying the dragon and releasing the life-giving waters of the world.

Ancient Dragons

Above: This 9th-century Cambodian temple carving shows Indra triumphing over Vritra.

A slightly different version of the myth of Vritra is told in the Mahabharata, where Vritra is created by Indra's enemy Tvastr, to destroy him. The great dragon succeeds in swallowing Indra but with the help of other gods Indra is freed and Vritra is destroyed.

Chapter I

Above: Leviathan faces off with God, in an engraving by Gustav Doré for *La Grand Bible de Tours* (1866).

Dragons of the Old Testament

Dragons and monstrous serpents haunt the Old Testament. The serpent in the Garden of Eden, though not explicitly dragon-like itself, formed the prototype for the long Christian and ultimately Western tradition of reptilian monsters as the embodiment of evil.

The idea of the dragon as a terrifying 'king of the beasts' owes much to the dramatic description of Leviathan, from the Book of Job. Leviathan was a creature of the deep ocean, and although often understood as a whale or sea monster, the graphic account of its attributes with which God regales Job suggests something closer to a dragon. God warns of how its 'circuit of teeth [are] a horror', how its scaly hide 'is like molten shields', and, strikingly, how 'Flames stream from its mouth . . . smoke pours from its nostrils. . . . Its breath sets coals ablaze.'

A third type of serpent-dragon monster is found in the Book of Daniel, where the prophet has an encounter with a serpent-monster (translated by Greek scribes as *drakōn*). Daniel proves to a Babylonian king that the dragon his priests worship is not divine, by killing it with a cake made from pitch, fat and hair, which causes its belly to burst, recalling the fate of Tiamat.

Chapter I

The Roman *Dracone*

∽

The Romans embraced the Greek tradition of the *drakōn* as a colourful adjunct to popular myths, but also maintained a tradition of dragons as real creatures. The most influential account of zoological dragons was that of Pliny the Elder (*c.*23–79 CE), the Roman statesman and encyclopaedist, who wrote of the lethal antagonism between dragon and elephant in India: 'the dragon . . . is perpetually at war with the elephant, and is itself so enormous in size, as easily to envelop the elephant with . . . its coils'. Dragons, Pliny said, were cunning and deadly, lying in wait to ambush their prey, striking up the elephant's trunk or sucking blood from behind its ear.

Pliny was confident in the dragon's existence because he was aware of a popular story dating from the First Punic War (256–241 BCE), when Roman soldiers campaigning in North Africa had encountered a serpentine dragon at the Bagrada River (in modern-day Tunisia). According to a thrilling, though not contemporary, account by the Roman author Silius Italicus, the colossal serpent – 'a deadly monster . . . whose like scarce any generation of man can see again' – issued forth from a noisome cavern, where it

Ancient Dragons

Above: Medieval bestiary illustration of Pliny's famous assertion that the elephant and the *dracone* are mortal enemies.

liked to devour prides of lions and herds of cattle. The Roman commander Regulus rallied his men to assault it with cavalry and war machines, and after a terrific battle it was felled. The account relates: 'The serpent's eyes flashed horrible fire; his erected crest towered over tall tree tops . . . towering above the frightened men with swollen neck [he] delighted in crushing them beneath his huge weight.' Just as the beast's forked tongue was flickering 'over the rump of the general's horse', the soldiers' javelins, arrows and ballistae bolts found their mark.

Regulus brought the remains back to Rome where, according to Pliny, 'its skin and jaws were preserved in a temple' until around 150 BCE. As with their Greek prototypes, these Roman dragons closely resembled snakes, but had some extra quality that distinguished them from mere *serpens*.

Inspirations and Analogues

The ubiquity of dragons in culture across the world and throughout history begs the question, where does the idea of the dragon come from? Ancient and medieval writers assumed that such a beast genuinely existed, although tellingly it always lived somewhere else. Pliny placed them in India. Islamic scholar al-Masudi (*c*.896–956) believed they lived in the Atlantic Ocean. But if we discount as fantasy the prospect that dragons exist or ever did, we are left with a puzzle: Why does everyone know about a creature that no one could ever have encountered?

Old bones
An obvious potential inspiration must be the closest thing Earth has come to real dragons: dinosaurs and similar prehistoric reptiles. Like dragons, they are giant, fearsome lizards, with heads full of teeth, horns and ridges; some with wings. Perhaps dinosaur fossils inspired human fantasies? The imaginative impact of chancing across, say, the fossilized skull of a *T. rex* would be considerable. But is there evidence that this has ever happened?

Historical examples apparently illustrating this dynamic include a story told by Pliny the Elder, of how Roman statesman Marcus Aemilius Scaurus brought back from Joppa in Judaea (modern-day Jaffa), the

Above: Engraving of possible dragon inspirations, the *Ichthyosaur* and the *Pliosaur*, from 1863.

petrified bones of a giant marine beast. Since Joppa was said to have been where Perseus rescued Andromeda and slew the Cetus, by petrifying it with the head of Medusa, they were believed to be the bones of the sea-dragon itself. A medieval variant of the 'fossils interpreted as dragon bones' trope is the Lindwurm of Klagenfurt in Austria, a dragon slain by a local hero in the thirteenth century, the skull of which was preserved in the town hall and, in 1582, used as the model for a statue of the supposed wurm. In fact the skull was that of a prehistoric woolly rhinoceros, while the bones of the Cetus of Joppa were probably those of a whale.

Lizard kings

Even if we accept that some dragon legends were inspired by fossils, this does not explain the prevalence and popularity of dragons in such regions as Scandinavia, where fossils are unlikely to have been observed. Perhaps living reptiles might be a source of inspiration. The Komodo dragon, for instance, is a ferocious, venomous scaly monster, which can reach more than 3 metres (10 feet) in length and weigh up to 166 kilograms (366 pounds). Although it inhabits only a few islands in Indonesia, other types of monitor lizard can be found from Africa through Oceania. But their range does not include Europe, and they are hardly an exact match for either Western or Eastern conceptions of dragons.

It may be that there is no single inspiration for the dragon. Like most monsters, dragons are hybrid creatures, combining aspects of snakes, lizards, crocodiles, ferocious mammals, sea creatures and flying beasts. What is common across all human cultures is the alchemical power of the imagination, combining primal fears, travellers' tales of exotic creatures and a taste for fantasy to generate tropes and archetypes that are passed on and elaborated through the generations. Some versions of the dragon — probably one closer to a snake than the modern, Western iteration — must have been one of the earliest of human memes: a meme that has evolved ever since.

Opposite: The dragon is a conceptual hybrid that draws on aspects of creatures as diverse as the monitor lizard (in an 1854 illustration) and the armoured rhinoceros (in an engraving of 1657).

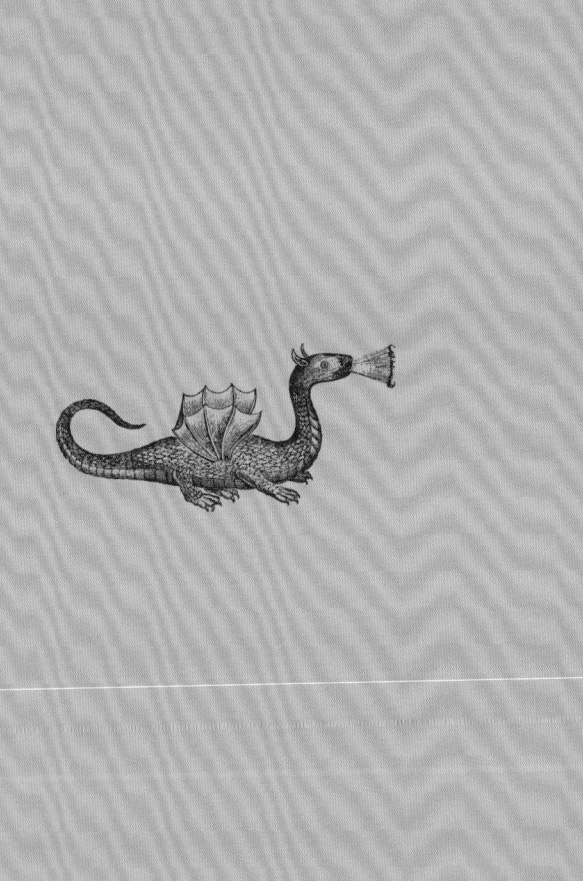

Chapter II

≈

Eastern Dragons

≈

Dragons of East and
Southeast Asia

Chapter II

The cultures of East and Southeast Asia have a very different dragon tradition from the West, one which dates back to the origins of civilisation in the region. In a remarkable burial of the Yangshao culture, on the North China Plain, dating to around 4000 BCE, the remains of a man were interred between two mosaic animals. One is probably a tiger, while the other resembles a dragon. By the time of Shang China (c.1766–1122 BCE), the character signifying *long*, the Chinese term commonly translated as dragon, appears on oracle bones, and dragon images were widespread in the material culture of the period; they are probably the most common ornamental motif of the era. Dragons have been found on bronzes, lacquers, bone carvings and jades from the Shang and Zhou era (c.1046–256 BCE), and probably decorated royal and priestly robes, and temple and palace interiors. The dragon continues to be the most widely represented symbol in Chinese art.

These dragons of East and Southeast Asia are elemental creatures typically associated with water, winds and clouds. They are shapeshifters, divinities, bringers of good fortune, symbols of imperial power and givers of gifts. 'None of the animals is so wise as the dragon', wrote the Chinese scholar Lu Dian (1042–1102 CE), 'His blessing power is not a false one. He can be smaller than small, bigger than big, higher than high and lower than low.'

Above: Chinese dragon medallion, 16th century. In the Ming dynasty, members of the imperial family wore robes decorated with such medallions, signifier of their association with the *long*, the Chinese term meaning dragon.

Chapter II

The Chinese *Long*

∞

It has been proposed that Eastern dragons – and Chinese ones in particular – should not be called by the Western name, but only by the Chinese term *long* (pronounced with a long 'o', and hence sometimes anglicized as *lung*), in recognition of their very different characteristics and associations. Yet there are some obvious points of comparison, such as their connection to water and rivers, and the fact that, like the Western dragon, the *long* is a composite beast. A classic description by the Han dynasty scholar Wang Fu (*c.*150 CE), explains that, 'The dragon's horns resemble those of a stag, his head that of a camel, his eyes those of a demon, his neck that of a snake, his belly that of a clam, his scales those of a carp, his claws those of an eagle, his feet those of a tiger, his ears those of a cow.'

The *long* may be ultimately derived from the Tiamat myth of ancient Mesopotamia, by way of cultural transmission across southern or central Asia, but there are several other theories. China is a rich source of fossils, many of which indeed came to be known as dragon bones, used in traditional medicine. Chinese alligators, now an endangered species, were once widespread in the swamps and rivers of prehistoric

Eastern Dragons

Above: Detail of a colour-glaze tile dragon from the 18th-century Nine Dragon Wall of the Forbidden City in Beijing.

Overleaf: A Chinese handscroll illustration showing a *long* dragon coiling through the air above cloud-wracked mountains.

and ancient China; perhaps they were an inspiration? A popular theory amongst Chinese academics is that the hybrid nature of the dragon represented the combination of the various animal totems of the different peoples of early China, and hence was an emblem of the foundational unity of the Chinese state.

Chapter II

Above: Early 19th-century Qing dynasty depiction of the Dragon King, in human form, mastering his watery domain.

The Dragon King

Dragons feature heavily in the mythic history of China. Gonggong, the Black Dragon, knocked down one of the pillars holding up the sky and caused a great flood. The mythic hero Huangdi, the Yellow Emperor, overcame the god-monster Chiyou by sending a winged dragon to cut off his head. Yuhuang, the Jade Emperor, was often depicted as a dragon, born from the corpse of his father.

Perhaps the most popular mythic incarnation was the Dragon King, a wise and magical being who lived in a palace beneath the sea. In Chinese Taoist myth the Eight Immortals come into conflict with him when one drops a musical instrument into the ocean, and they battle to recover it. The Dragon King could also be helpful and generous. In one Vietnamese folk tale a student rescues a turtle from nets, and discovers a beautiful princess in its shell. She is the daughter of the Dragon King, who helps the student pass his exams. In Vietnamese myth, the Dragon King was the progenitor of the first ruling dynasty, after a Vietnamese hero married a princess of the Dragon King's family, who gave birth to Lac Long Quang, also known as the Dragon King.

Chapter II

Japanese Dragons

~

Like their Chinese forebears, Japanese dragons are mystical elemental beings, usually linked to water and clouds. As in other Eastern kingdoms, the Japanese imperial family claim direct descent from a dragon: Ryūjin, the dragon god of the sea.

Japan has many tales of dragons and heroes. The oldest surviving text from Japan, the eighth-century *Kojiki* (*Records of Ancient Matters*), tells the story of Susanowo, a god who defeats an eight-headed serpent-dragon by getting it drunk. When he cuts it his sword breaks on an object embedded in its flesh, which turns out to be the legendary blade Grass-Cutter, one of the three sacred treasures of the imperial regalia. In Japanese legend the Dragon King lives in a fabulous undersea palace, Ryūgū. He features in the classic 'Tale of Tawara Tōda', in which a brave warrior comes to the aid of the Dragon King and slays a monstrous centipede, for which he is rewarded with an always-full bag of rice. In a variation on the Vietnamese tale, a fisherman rescues a turtle and is rewarded with the affections of the Dragon King's daughter, but when he insists on returning home from Ryūgū, to care for his parents, he discovers that centuries have passed, and ages abruptly.

Eastern Dragons

Above: Legendary pearl-diver princess Tamatori is pursued by Ryūjin and his marine minions in this woodblock illustration.

Chapter II

Dragon Culture

~

Dragons have left their mark on culture from Korea to Borneo, appearing in a multitude of guises. One of the most colourful is the dragon dance, probably originating in the Han era (202 BCE–220 CE) as a propitiation ritual for ancestors but today celebrated to bring good luck and ward off evil (apotropaic). In a dragon dance each dancer controls a joint of the dragon's body or the head; odd numbers of joints are considered propitious. Typically another dancer holds a *longzhu*, or dragon pearl, on a pole in front of the head, guiding the dance.

Dragon dances spread along with Chinese culture – for instance, they are often performed in Singapore – and they may have inspired traditional dances in Indonesia. The Barong dance, especially popular in Bali, re-enacts the myth of the Barong, a dragon or lion king who defeats the evil witch-queen Rangda. Chinese influence, probably via imported decorated vessels brought by Chinese traders, is almost certainly the inspiration for the dragon motifs found in the long verandahs of traditional houses of the Kayan and Kenyah people in Borneo.

Dragon dances are associated with Chinese New Year festivals. Another dragon festival is Duanwu Jie,

Eastern Dragons

Above: A 19th-century print of a Chinese dragon dance; note the dancer with the *longzhu* at the head of the procession.

Overleaf: Painting of a dragon boat race from Hangzhou, Zhejiang Province, China.

the Dragon Boat festival, celebrated on the fifth day of the fifth month of the Chinese lunar calendar (possibly because the number '5' was considered inauspicious, and the festival is intended to be propitious and apotropaic). Long, narrow boats decorated with dragons are raced by teams armed with paddles, while celebrants eat sticky-rice balls wrapped in bamboo leaves.

Dragons All Over?

Numerous examples in this book, from myths and legends from around the world, have already attested that the dragon is a culturally promiscuous creature. But is it universal? Can dragons be found in every culture or society on Earth? The answer is that it depends on what counts as a dragon. Dragons by their nature are hybrid creatures, composed of elements of different beasts, and, as we have seen (see page 36), the mixture varies through time and across continents. Accordingly translators have a loose remit when it comes to rendering the names of mythical beasts as 'dragons'. With this in mind, what far-flung dragons can we discover? This book covers in detail dragon traditions from ancient Mesopotamia, the Mediterranean, Europe, and East and Southeast Asia. What of Africa, the Americas, Oceania and South Asia?

Naga

The Naga of South and Southeast Asia are sometimes described as dragons. They are semidivine serpent people, sometimes snake-human hybrids, which share many characteristics with dragons, particularly those of the Eastern tradition. They are associated with water, dwelling in lakes and rivers, and generating clouds and rain; they can bring good fortune; and they are declared as divine ancestors of royalty. The Khmer of Cambodia, for instance, claim descent from a Naga princess.

Above: Modern reconstruction of the Piasa bird petroglyph of Alton, Illinois; the 17th-century original version was destroyed.

Thunderbirds and feathered serpents

Native American myths and legends feature several dragon-like entities. Mesoamerican gods such as Quetzalcóatl (a.k.a. Kukulcán) are described as feathered serpents. As with the Yellow Dragon, Huanglong, Quetzalcóatl was a culture hero who taught humans the art of writing. North American Indians had legends of mighty winged creatures called thunderbirds, sometimes interpreted as dragons. One of the strangest Native American monsters is the legendary Piasa bird, a dragon-like beast known only from a seventeenth-century description and later reconstructions of a now destroyed rock painting by the Algonquian Illiniweks of the Mississippi River Valley. French explorer Father

Above: Detail from a pre-Columbian Aztec codex showing the feathered serpent god Quetzalcóatl devouring a human being.

James Marquette, who claimed to have seen it in 1673, described the painted figure as having 'the face of a man' but with 'green, red, and black scales, and a tail so long it passed around the body, over the head, and between the legs'.

Rainbow serpents and Taniwha

Many African societies have myths and legends of supernatural serpent-creatures, which could be interpreted as dragons. The Ninki Nanka, which presages death, is a creature of West African folklore said to be a hybrid of snake, crocodile and other beasts. The mythology of the Dahomey people of West Africa features the rainbow serpent Aido Hwedo, a cosmic snake similar to the Norse world serpent. Its colouring evokes Australian Aboriginal myths of the Rainbow Serpent, a divine culture hero responsible for shaping the landscape and teaching humans the art of painting. Rainbow serpents also occur in Yoruba and Congolese myths. According to the epics of the Soninke and Fulbe people, the ancient kingdom of Ghana was plagued by a 'great snake' called Bida that was propitiated with a maiden sacrifice until a hero dispatched it.

Even remote Pacific islands have dragon myths. The Maori of New Zealand have the Taniwha, a shape-shifting water monster often translated as 'dragon', and typically associated with rulers. An old Maori idiom for the death of a chief is '*Unuhia noatia te taniwha i te rua*', or 'withdrawn now is the dragon from his lair'.

Chapter III

∽

Wyrms

∽

Dragons of the
Northern Lands

Chapter III

Alongside the Mediterranean and Near Eastern traditions of dragons, epitomized by Greek and Roman serpent-dragons, a northern European tradition of Norse dragons was characterised primarily by what the Old Norse called *ormr* (*wyrm* in Old English). These wyrms were also serpent-dragons, given, like their southern counterparts, to skulking in caverns and haunting rivers, lakes and seas. They might have legs, but they did not fly. They breathed and exuded poison. But Old Norse had also borrowed the term *dreki*, from Graeco-Roman roots, to describe dragons that flew and might breathe fire.

Primarily in Britain, the Norse tradition inspired Celtic variants, which encompassed both wyrms and drakes, while Germany fostered a Teutonic tradition, which retold many of the same tales. It was via these British and Germanic legendaria that the modern Western archetype of the dragon became established, in particular through Jacob Grimm's 1835 collection *Teutonic Mythology*, which featured a whole section devoted to dragons. The other seminal influence was professor of Anglo-Saxon, J. R. R. Tolkien, who drew inspiration from the dragons of Norse legend and Beowulf to fashion the greatest of literary dragons, as well as arguing in his scholarship for the central importance of the dragon in European culture. Via Grimm and Tolkien, the characteristics of the northern dragon – jealously guarding hoards of treasure, stalking blasted heaths, vying with sword-wielding heroes – became the stereotypical features of all dragons.

Above: Illustration from a 17th-century Icelandic manuscript, showing the Midgard Serpent being baited with a bull's head on a hook.

Chapter III

Above: Henry Fuseli's 1790 painting *Thor Battering the Midgard Serpent* – note the cringing Hymer in the bow.

Overleaf: In this late-19th-century illustration of Ragnarok, by Norwegian artist Louis Moe, the Midgard Serpent lashes the seas into an apocalyptic tide.

Jörmungandr, the Midgard Serpent

In Norse myth the union of Loki, god of mischief, with Angerboda, a giantess, produced monstrous progeny including the serpent-dragon Jörmungandr. Unable to control him, Odin, king of the gods, threw him into the ocean, where he grew to such monstrous dimensions that he encircled the whole of Midgard, the Norse name for the Earthly plane, and so was also known as the Midgard Serpent.

Thor had several run-ins with this colossal snake-monster, most notably his fishing trip with the giant Hymer, during which the thunder-god used an ox head as bait to snare Jörmungandr, and was only prevented from landing him when the cowardly giant cut the fishing line. Thor is also fated to meet Jörmungandr in the epic final battle of the Norse gods and the forces of darkness: Ragnarok. In the course of this, the writhings of the world-serpent will inundate the land with tsunami, and Thor and Jörmungandr will kill one another.

Cross-cultural comparisons point to similarities with tales such as Indra's battle with Vritra (see page 22), suggesting a very ancient ur-myth from which both traditions sprang.

Chapter III

Fafnir

The story of Fafnir the dragon and Sigurd the dragon-slayer is the most famous of the Norse dragon tales. It has been popular in both Scandinavian and Germanic literature and art, featuring in the thirteenth-century *Völsunga saga* and the German *Nibelungenlied* partly based on it, which in turn inspired Wagner's *Ring Cycle*. Fafnir was originally a man (or a dwarf or giant, depending on the version), corrupted by avarice and transformed into a monstrous wyrm, as he squatted on ill-gotten, cursed treasure. The treasure had been a blood price paid to redeem the death of a brother, and Fafnir had killed his father and made off with it. As with the dragon in Beowulf (see page 67), Fafnir reveals that, for the Norse, such a creature was a symbol of the corrupting power of greed, the flip side of the wealth and largesse that marked out great men.

In the story, Fafnir's brother Regin plots to get his hands on the treasure, to which end he mentors a heroic youth, Sigurd (Siegfried in Germanic versions). Schooled in valour and martial arts, Sigurd agrees to take on the dragon when Regin makes for him the sword

Opposite: Illustrator Arthur Rackham's unique take on the dragon Fafnir (1911) seems to draw inspiration from cave-dwelling amphibians as much as reptiles.

Chapter III

Above: A much older version of the myth of Sigurd killing Fafnir, from the medieval Hylestad Stave Church in Norway.

Gram ('Wrath'), forged from broken blades, which can cut through an anvil. As they approach the withered heath where Fafnir lurks and spreads his poison, Regin advises Sigurd to dig a pit and strike at the wyrm from below, but neglects to mention that the blood will be fatal. A mysterious stranger (Odin in disguise) advises Sigurd to dig other trenches to drain away the blood, and

Sigurd successfully kills the beast, though not before Fafnir engages him in a dangerous conversation, seeking to learn his destroyer's name so that he may curse him. At first Sigurd maintains his anonymity, but eventually lets slip the fatal information.

The dragon dies but the drama is not yet done, for Regin returns and asks Sigurd to roast for him Fafnir's heart. When the hero accidentally tastes some of the dragon's blood he acquires the power to understand the speech of birds, and is warned that Regin plans to kill him. Chopping off Regin's head, Sigurd takes the dragon's hoard, including a cursed golden ring, and rides off to further adventures, but is fated to a terrible doom thanks to the dragon and the ring.

Fafnir is a classic wyrm of the northern tradition. He has no wings, and recalls earlier Graeco-Roman serpent-dragons as he slithers and writhes, exudes and breathes poison, despoils the land through his noxious emissions and makes the earth tremble as he passes. It is also interesting to note that in this tale the hero triumphs through stratagem (and wise counsel), rather than force of arms.

The tale of Fafnir was clearly a great inspiration for Tolkien, particularly for his conception of the dragon Smaug in *The Hobbit*. Direct influences include the dragon squatting on its hoard of treasure; the mesmerising power of dragon's speech, and the importance of the hero not revealing their name; talking birds; reforged swords; and, of course, a cursed ring.

Chapter III

Mester Stoorworm

∾

The Viking outpost of the Orkneys, an archipelago just off the north coast of Scotland, is home to a distinctive variation of the Scandinavian wyrm legend, namely the tale of Mester Stoorworm, 'the largest, the first and the father of all the stoorworms'. Resembling Jörmungandr, this serpent-monster was a colossal marine creature. Its poison breath 'could kill every living creature on which it fell, and could wither up everything that grew', according to the folklorist Traill Dennison. It was said that the enormous breaths of the monster accounted for the huge tides that swept back and forth in the seas around Orkney. When roused it would rest its head on the mainland and loll out its 'awful tongue, hundreds of miles long', which 'would sweep whole towns, trees and hills into the sea'.

In the Orcadian folktale, Mester Stoorworm is defeated by the dragon-slayer Assipattle, a name with similar roots to Cinderella. Assipattle is a feckless dreamer, called into action to take on the monster, which he defeats by being sucked into its maw and poking a smouldering cinder into its liver. The worm burns up, and in its agonies spews out teeth

Wyrms

Above: The Scar Dragon plaque of *c.*1000 CE shows how medieval Orcadians might have conceived Mester Stoorworm.

that become the Scottish islands, while its contorted body becomes Iceland.

The tale has many similarities with the Celtic dragon of Cnoc na Cnoimh, of Sutherland in northern Scotland; and the Linton Worm, in the Scottish Borders, both killed by heroes wielding burning peat on the end of a lance or spear. All recall the trope of Daniel and the dragon, from the Bible (see page 24).

Beowulf and the Barrow Guardian

Beowulf is an epic poem in Old English, written *c.*700–1000 CE, which tells of the eponymous Norse hero, who sails from Sweden to Denmark to help rid a lord of the ogre, Grendel, who is plaguing his hall. Beowulf dispatches the ogre, and returns home to reign as a mighty king for decades, until called to take on a dragon ravaging his lands. The dragon has been roused because a thief stole a single cup from its hoard, and Beowulf gives his life to defeat it, in a titanic struggle that sees him sustain fatal wounds.

The unnamed dragon of Beowulf is one of the most significant in the Western tradition, mainly thanks to its influence on Tolkien, but it also represents a synthesis of Norse and Christian dragons. It is one of the first depicted as flying and breathing fire, and is evocatively described as 'hoard-guard', 'wide flier', 'ring-coiling' and 'barrow-guardian' (a barrow being a burial mound). For Anglo-Saxons, the dragon, which hoarded its gold for centuries, was a perversion of the natural order, in which treasure was to be shared out by its owner.

Opposite: Beowulf and the dragon lie dead, having taken each other's lives in a climactic battle.

Dragon Habitats

The modern dragon is a creature of caverns and wastelands, mainly thanks to the influence of the Norse tradition, but ancient dragons were strongly associated with water, and, in the East, with clouds, vapours and the air. These different habitat traditions may appear to be at odds, but they have important symbolic aspects in common.

Water monsters
From Tiamat and Vritra, to Greek *cetae* and the Roman Bagrada dragon, to the Norse Jörmungandr, water was for long the essential element associated with dragons. Even those dragons associated with caverns and wastelands, like Fafnir, would often be encountered while at or on their way to their watering stations. Watery places, including rivers, springs, marshes and shores, are liminal zones; monsters that dwell in them exist on or beyond the threshold of the natural world. In many cultures, water was associated with the underworld, the land of the dead, while in ancient myths of widely differing cultures, water was an emblem of chaos, and the dragon was an agent or incarnation of disorder. Defeat of the dragon by a hero represents the

Opposite: The Psalter World Map of *c*.1270, a copy of which probably hung in the bedchamber of Henry III, shows a pair of dragons at the base of the world.

triumph of order over chaos, civilisation over the wild, life over death.

Going underground

In many dragon tales there is an elision between the watery and the subterranean, as in nature where water often comes from the ground, in springs or caverns; disappears into the ground, in sinkholes or cave systems; or fills pits and holes. Perhaps this is the original route by which dragons became associated with caves and pits, or perhaps the reasons are more obvious: as creatures of terror and darkness, dragons would naturally issue forth from the underworld, the realm of death and darkness. Certainly in the Norse tradition of dragons as hoard-guardians, it makes sense for them to lurk within barrows, hollow hills and caverns, wherein they can gather and conceal their treasure. This tradition of dragon habitat reaches its apotheosis in the name of the most famous of fantasy games, *Dungeons & Dragons*.

Into the wasteland

Dragons were also associated with wastes, blasted heaths, remote mountains and wilderness. Sometimes this was because they themselves laid waste to the land, through their toxic emanations, as with Fafnir, the dragon fought by St George, or even the Bagrada River dragon. The wasteland offers another symbolic opposition to the human values of civilisation and order. In the classic St-George-style Christian narrative, the dragon menaces the people of a city; an intrusion into the tamed and civilised human zone by the destructive, chaotic force of savage nature. Wilderness as a habitat also makes sense in the context of what scholars and writers believed about the reality of dragons, which were always said to live just beyond the known world, in the border regions marked with 'Here be dragons' (although in fact the only known use of the Latin phrase *Hic Sunt Dracones* is on the 1504 Hunt-Lenox globe).

Air power

The Eastern tradition, while often featuring water-dwelling dragons (in particular the Dragon King in his submarine palace), offers an alternative habitat, in the airy realm. Chinese dragons are often associated with clouds, rain and the wind. They represent the beneficial aspects of water: life-giving, drought-relieving, crop-watering. By extension these airy dragons, although they can be fierce and storm-bringing, are generally regarded as auspicious beings. They also hint at the possible animistic roots of dragon-belief, linking dragons with the otherworldly power of lightning, the tempest and the whirlwind.

Overleaf: The 1539 Carta Marina map of Swedish cleric Olaus Magnus, is famous for its sea monsters, including a wyrm-like beast off the coast of Norway.

Chapter IV

Christian Dragons

Saints, Serpents
and Symbolism

Chapter IV

Dragons come into the Christian era via two avenues. The first is the Bible; dragons feature sparingly in the Old Testament (see page 24), but in the New Testament they provide some of the most striking and vivid phrases and imagery. Revelation 20:2 prophesies an apocalyptic 'great red dragon with seven heads and ten horns', against which Michael and his angels will do battle, and offers the key association: 'the dragon, that old serpent, which is the Devil, and Satan'. The iconography of demons and the devil thus became the iconography of the dragon; just as Satan was depicted in his fallen angel guise with wings contorted into those of a bat, a creature of the night, so the dragon acquired bat-like wings.

The second avenue was the adoption by early Church scholars of classical models and authorities, in particular Isidore of Seville's appropriation of Pliny's claims about the dragon, although he in turn was following in the footsteps of earlier Christian writers such as Augustine. Christians would put their own slant on the lore of the ancients by interpreting the natural world in the light of their faith, reading in the Book of Creation affirmations of the dispensation of Christianity, and writing this into their own books, specifically the *liber bestiarium*, or bestiaries. They also appropriated pagan narratives of heroes battling dragons to juice up their hagiographies.

Christian Dragons

Above: St Michael the Archangel dispatching a Satanic hydra-like dragon.

Chapter IV

Augustine and Gregory

The Church Fathers – distinguished scholars of the early Christian church – had plenty to say about dragons. Augustine of Hippo (354–430 CE) wrote extensively about them, and appeared to believe they were real creatures. 'As for dragons, which lack feet, they are said to take their rest in caves, and to soar up into the air', he discoursed, admitting that they 'are not too easy to come across' but going on to explain how they 'favour watery habitats . . . create major atmospheric disturbance . . . [and] are the largest creatures on earth'. Augustine's belief in the literal reality of dragons may owe something to his personal encounter with a tooth, 'on the beach at Utica [which] I saw with my own eyes . . . the tooth of a giant' (probably a fossilized whale or mammoth tooth). Augustine's view of dragons was as both avatars of evil and evidence of the majesty of God's creation: 'when you consider the dragons, regard the Maker of the dragon, the Creator . . . and say, Great is the Lord who made these'.

Pope Gregory the Great, in his influential *Dialogues on the Miracles of the Italian Fathers* (written *c.*592), related several tales of errant monks literally caught in

Christian Dragons

Above: A 13th-century miniature of the Hellmouth: monstrous heads frame a portal to Hell, in which can be seen a many-headed dragon.

the coils of temptation and evil, in the form of dragons. A monk of Ton Galaton, for instance, who had been secretly eating when meant to be fasting, lamented, 'now I have been given to a dragon to be devoured. It has already coiled around my knees and feet . . . and gulps down my spirit'. Gregory's tales helped create the imagery of the dragon-like Hellmouth, gobbling up the souls of the damned.

Chapter IV

Above: Raphael's version of the George and dragon legend (*c.* 1506), is a cabinet miniature that was probably made as a gift for an emissary of King Henry VII of England.

Saint Versus Dragon

In Graeco-Roman literature the tale of a battle between a dragon and a hero was a popular motif, and Christian hagiography is replete with similar narratives. The earliest example is from the purported prison diary of Perpetua, a Christian woman jailed for her faith in 203 CE, who recorded a vision of the devil in the guise of a dragon guarding a bronze ladder to heaven, which she subdued by invoking Christ.

Of the hundreds of tales that followed, many were conversion narratives, in which pagan populations were brought to Christianity by the triumph of the saint, in some cases over a pagan dragon-cult. The fourth-century Acts of Philip relates how 'a sudden wind arose . . . and out of it ran a great smoky dragon, with a black back, and a belly like coals of brass giving off sparks'. Faced with this horror, the object of veneration by a serpent cult in Ophiorhyme (Heriapolis), the Apostle Philip and his companions invoked the power of God, and a flash of lightning withered the dragon. Another popular tale was that of Margaret the Virgin, swallowed by Satan in the form of a dragon, only to burst forth from its belly by burning it with a cross. The most famous saintly dragon-slayer was, of course, St George (see overleaf).

Chapter IV

Saint George

～

George of Syria was probably an apocryphal figure but he is said to have been a Roman soldier martyred in Diocletian's persecutions of the early fourth century CE. He would go on to become one of the most popular of all Christian saints, with cults from the Middle East to Britain. In the Middle Ages the tale of his battle with the dragon became popular with Crusaders, who brought it back to Europe, and it was later made even more famous by inclusion in the *Golden Legend*, Caxton's late-fifteenth-century version of which became one of the first printed English-language bestsellers.

The story was probably a conflation of George's legend with that of Perseus and Andromeda, in which the hero slayed the dragon-like Ethiopian Cetus. In George's version, the dragon is laying waste to the countryside with its poison breath, and the people are about to appease it with the sacrifice of a princess when George pierces it with his lance and subdues it with the maiden's girdle. He offers to dispatch it if the people will embrace Christianity – the kingdom is duly converted.

This battle became one of the most popular of Christian images, but since similar triumphs are ascribed

Above: This late-medieval Croatian illuminated missal shows the fabulously crested St George dispatching a flying dragon.

Overleaf: Paolo Uccello's iconic portrayal of this topic (c.1470), is notable for its striking and unusual two-legged dragon.

to St Michael, St Margaret and more than forty other saints of the Western church, it may not always be clear who is depicted. The dragon in this context is an allegory for evil and the devil's influence, and so the image of the valiant knight conquering the repulsive serpent becomes a representation of the virtues of muscular Christianity.

sunt duo quorum unus s[ci]uitatem ser[m]dat. Alt[er] fecundi st[er]lem
facit. In tesalia duo sunt flumina. et uno bibentes oues nig[ra]s fi-
unt. aut albas. ex utroq[ue] uarias. fluu[iu]s p[re]n lacus iuxta maximos
uues gignit. Reatinis paludis aq[ua]s uisitor[um] ungulas m[ar]mora-
ri dicit[ur]. In asfaltide lacu iudee m[er]gi n[on] p[otest] quicq[ue] a[n]i[m]am
h[abe]t. Jn india dissiden uocat[ur] stagnu[m] n[ic]h[il] inatat[ur] s[ed] o[mn]ia m[er]-
gunt[ur]. At co[n]t[ra] in alce lacu[m] p[ro]pe damum ui o[mn]ia fluitant nich[il] m[er]-
git[ur]. Cyrsidis fons in frigia saxa g[e]n[er]at. In achaia aq[ua] p[er]fluit ex
saxis. Stix appellata q[uod] illico potata intersicit. Selo amnis stagnu[m] sicile tetro odore auig[e]t p[ro]ximantes.

Draco maior cu[n]ctor[um] serpentium siue a[n]i[m]antiu[m] om[n]ium
sup[er] t[er]ram. hunc greci draconta uocant. un[de] [et] diriuatum
est in latinum. ut draco diceret[ur]. Qui sepe. a spelu[n]cis abstrictus

Christian Dragons

Medieval Bestiaries

∞

Medieval *liber bestiarium*, a.k.a. bestiaries, gave accounts of animals and sometimes other aspects of the natural world (e.g., rocks) along with their Christian allegorical significance. The dragon, as one of the most colourful and striking of beasts, was a favourite subject. Following the Bible, bestiaries explicitly compared the dragon to the devil, as for instance in the Bodleian Library MS 764 bestiary: 'The dragon is like the devil, the fairest of all serpents, who often leaves his cave to rush into the air; the air glows because of him, because the devil rises from his abyss and transforms himself into an angel of light, deceiving fools with hopes of vainglory and human pleasures.'

The claim, which can be traced back to Pliny (see page 26) that dragons lie in wait for elephants and coil around them, is repurposed to illustrate the ways of the devil: 'its strength does not rest in its teeth but in its tail, because having lost all power, the devil can only deceive with lies. It lurks on the paths which elephants use because the devil lays the coils of sin in the path

Opposite: Dragon attacking an elephant, from a medieval bestiary.

of all who make their way towards heaven and kills them when they are suffocated with sin.' Note the link with the imagery in the stories of Gregory the Great (see page 78).

Another claim made in bestiaries linked the dragon with the panther. The latter was believed to be a symbol of Christ, and it was said that after eating a large meal, the panther falls asleep for several days. Upon waking it roars, breathing forth a heavenly odour so sweet that it attracts all the other animals (just as the virtuous are drawn to the teachings of Christ), except for the dragon, which flees to cower beneath the earth, as the devil cowers in the face of God.

Bestiaries also offer plenty of fascinating lore about dragons. For instance, as they flew overhead, they were said to rain down urine that would petrify human skin and cause affected body parts to fall off. Dragons were said to fear the peridexion tree (a legendary fruit tree of the Indies), avoiding its shadow, so doves loved to roost in the trees, knowing they would be safe.

Later in the Middle Ages, bestiaries were superseded by more ambitious encyclopaedic works, but these still found room for dragons. The encyclopaedia of Thomas of Cantimpré, for example, explained that some ingenious and plucky individuals had invented air travel by capturing dragons, lashing themselves to the backs of the beasts and being carried at speed to faraway places. Transoceanic travel, however, had proved problematic, for the creatures tired and fell into the sea. Thomas

Christian Dragons

Above: Gold-leaf illumination of the peridexion tree, from the early-13th-century Oxford Bestiary.

also gave a scientifically credible version of the folkloric trick for killing a dragon, advising filling the belly of a slaughtered calf with quicklime (highly reactive calcium oxide), so that when a dragon takes the bait it effectively sets fire to its own innards.

Dragon Attributes

The stereotypical dragon of today is a composite of attributes accrued over a long cultural evolution. Reptilian features are foremost, reflecting the dragon's primary origin as a sort of super snake, hence its sinuous body and long tail. In Christian interpretations, the tail was freighted with its own significance, recalling the serpent in the Garden of Eden, and becoming the main weapon of the dragon, constricting prey – whether elephants or sinners – in its coils. From reptiles the dragon also acquired its scaly skin, which comes to the fore in Norse tales as an (almost) impenetrable armour. Only the wise, learned and skilled can find the chink in this armour, the fatal flaw that dooms the monster.

Wings are non-reptilian features but the ancient Greeks and Romans had a long tradition of flying snakes, which recurs in odd places, such as Welsh folklore, as well as the heraldic amphiptere of medieval Europe. Illustrations for legends of Alexander the Great showed him battling dragons with feathered wings, but typically the dragon's wings may owe more to the bat wings that Christian artists imagined belonging to Satan, the fallen angel. As well as feathers there have been some famous furry dragons, such as the Peluda (see page 103).

Above: The Dragon and the Beast, after a miniature from a 12th-century manuscript. In translations of the Apocalypse, the terms 'serpent' and 'dragon' are used interchangeably.

Bad breath and long life

Following Biblical associations with flames and smoke, and the influential dragon of Beowulf, fire-breathing is a core attribute of dragons in the modern conception, but traditionally they were more associated with poisonous/noxious breath. It was long believed that disease is propagated via the air, and the miasmatic exudations of the dragon could thus be pestilential, helping to explain the link between dragons and malarial swamps and marshes. For example, the people of Dunster, in England's marshy Somerset levels, were terrorised by a pestilential dragon until it was banished by St Carantoc. Dragons themselves were evidently immune to their emanations; in both Eastern and Norse traditions they were fantastically long-lived, perhaps even immortal. In several traditions dragons borrowed from their reptilian antecedents regenerative abilities.

Draconites

Perhaps the strangest feature attributed to dragons is the *draconite* (sometimes spelt *dracontite*) or dragon stone; a gemstone said to grow in the brain of the dragon, which could only be obtained if, in the words of Pliny, 'the head of the animal is cut off while it is alive'. Isidore of Seville, borrowing from Pliny, explained that 'bold men explore the cave of the dragons, and scatter there medicated grains to hasten their sleep, and thus cut off their heads while they are sunk in sleep, and take out the gems'. This legend probably derived from Indian tales about serpent stones:

Above: Alexander the Great fighting dragons, engraving after a miniature in the *Alexander Romance*, Burgundy, 13th century.

Overleaf: The dragon of the Apocalypse, complete with bat-like wings, from the 16th-century Luther Bible.

gems that give the snakes the power to find treasure. In Philostratus' third-century-CE *Life of Apollonius of Tyana* he describes how the Indians 'embroider golden runes on a scarlet cloak', and that together with 'much mysterious lore [that] is sung . . . the runes induce the dragon to stretch his neck out of his burrow and fall asleep [on the cloak]', whereupon the creature's head is lopped off. In nineteenth-century Cyprus enterprising traders counterfeited draconites and sold them as amulets to counter poison (akin to unicorn horns), while belief in snake stones supposedly persists to this day in parts of India.

Chapter V

Dragons of Fable and Folklore

Heroes, Tricks and Trophies

Chapter V

By the Middle Ages dragons were culturally ubiquitous, passing into folk culture and thus into folklore. A rich store of dragon-related folklore and fables exists in many cultures, but those of Europe are today the best known, partly thanks to the burst of scholarship and collecting sparked by the intertwined Romantic and Nationalist movements of the nineteenth century, which produced collections such as Grimms' *Märchen* (which featured a St George-style dragon battle in *The Two Brothers*).

The dragons of these tales are generally less impressive than those of earlier eras. This diminishing effect is neatly captured by a marginal seventeenth-century rhyme in a book about St George: 'To save a maid, St George a dragon slew; A pretty tale, if all that's told be true; Most say there are no dragons; and 'tis said; There was no George. Pray God there was a maid.'

Nonetheless folkloric dragons retain most of the typical features that had come to define the creature. According to a classic analysis of dragon fables by English folklorist Jacqueline Simpson, dragons are typically cave/water-dwelling, armoured with scales, equipped with wings and fiery/noxious breath, covet treasure and maidens and lay waste to entire locales. Folk tales about them include heroes of either storied noble lineage or crafty underdog status, involve an ingenious method of dispatching the dragon (such as spiked armour or an armoured barrel), and the citing of real-world objects (relics or local landmarks) as proof of the tale.

Dragons of Fable and Folklore

Above: Red and white dragons battle before King Vortigern, in a classic episode from British folklore.

Chapter V

The Lambton Worm

~

A classic example of dragon folklore is the tale of the Lambton Worm. The best-known version tells of how a young scion of Lambton Castle, in northeast England, skips church on a Sunday to go fishing, catches a loathsome creature and casually discards it in a well. Repenting of his sins he goes on Crusade, returning years later to find that his youthful sin has taken monstrous form in the shape of a Norse-style wyrm, which coils around Worm Hill, despoils the region of livestock, and is placated with troughs of milk. The monster has regenerative powers that make it seemingly impossible to defeat, but the knight dons a suit of spiked armour and battles the dragon in the river, slicing it into pieces that are washed away.

In more elaborate versions, the armour is dreamt up by a witch who demands as payment the life of the first being to greet the knight after his victory, and then curses him when he refuses to kill his father, so that thereafter no lord of Lambton would die in his bed. The tale encompasses several tropes of dragon and wider folklore: the advisory witch recalls both Odin's role in the tale of Sigurd and Fafnir (see page 60), and the payment demanded of the father in the story of Beauty and the Beast.

Above: The Lambton knight in his spiked armour prepares to take on the loathsome worm. The tale recapitulates many classic folkloric tropes.

Chapter V

The Tarasque

~

The town of Tarascon, in southern France, celebrates its fabled dragon with processions and effigies. Known as the Tarasque, it was a horrible hybrid monster described in the medieval legend of St Martha. In the dark forest along the river Rhone, Martha encountered a monster that was 'fatter than an ox, longer than a horse, with a lion's face and head, teeth as sharp as swords, a horse's mane, its back as sharp as an axe, bristling and piercing scales, six feet with bear's claws, a serpent's tail, and a shell on either side like a tortoise'.

Interrupting the dragon as it feasted upon a victim, Martha threw holy water on it and held up a cross. The Tarasque allowed itself to be bound with her girdle and led meekly back to town, whereupon the townsfolk gleefully beat it to death, but adopted its name for their town. Since the Middle Ages, the legend of the Tarasque has been celebrated by parading an articulated effigy, with five men hidden inside, who could make it dance and lunge. Townsfolk would attempt to snatch spikes from its hides while the Tarasque tried to knock them down. If it succeeded, the crowd would cry out 'A que ben fé! A que ben fé! La Tarascon a rou un bré!'

Dragons of Fable and Folklore

Above: The annual Tarasque parade could be violent, as shown in this engraving of a late-19th-century iteration.

('Oh that's well done! Oh that's well done! The Tarasque has smashed an arm!'). Nowadays, the procession is less violent and dangerous.

Possibly related is another French dragon, La Velue, a.k.a. 'the Hairy One' or 'the Shaggy Beast', noted for its green fur. It was defeated with a strike to its only weak spot, its tail. Thanks to its inclusion in Jorge Luis Borges's 1957 *Book of Imaginary Beings*, it is today better known by the Spanish translation of its name: the Peluda.

Chapter V

The Dragon of Wantley

~

Folklore tends to be less serious and more irreverent than myth or legend, and both heroes and dragons can become figures of fun in dragon fables. For instance, in mummers' plays (folk theatre performed by non-professionals, with its roots in medieval practice), the dragon is diminished to a pantomime figure, and sometimes even a comical turn. In the traditional *Oxfordshire St George Miracle Play*, a Victorian English continuation of a medieval custom, the dragon turns somersaults, speaks doggerel – 'Stand on head, stand on feet! Meat, meat, meat for to eat!' – and is comically poisoned by the doctor.

A particularly bawdy version of the classic dragon fable is the Dragon of Wantley (a.k.a. Wharncliff Lodge, Yorkshire), a burlesque that dates to at least the seventeenth century, printed as a popular song in 1685. In his armour, 'With spikes all about, not within but without', the hero, More of More-hall, defeats the dragon by kicking it with his spiked boot, whereupon the dragon complains, 'More of More-hall! Oh thou rascal! . . . with the thing at thy foot, thou hast pricked my assgut', and expires in undignified fashion: 'First on one knee, then on back tumbled he; So groan'd, kickt, farted and died.'

Above: More of More-hall – sporting armour familiar from the tale of the Lambton Worm (see page 100) – delivers the killing blow to the dragon's fundament.

Overleaf: Illustration from a broadsheet recounting the Dragon of Wantley fable, showing the beast mauling a hapless victim.

Supposedly a painting of the battle was kept at Wharncliff Lodge, while some boulders in the vicinity were said to be the only things the destructive dragon had left standing.

The Dragon of La Trinita

~

The folkloric archetypes of the dragon fable can be found in diverse countries and regions. A tale collected from a charcoal burner in rustic Tuscany, and reported in a 1910 edition of the journal *Folk-Lore*, contains many of the classic motifs. In the Tuscan hills, where the Friary of La Trinita was subsequently built, a dragon dwelt in a cavern, issuing forth to predate on livestock and even clergymen. The 'Great Duke Sforza' rode to battle the dragon, but the beast withdrew. The hero tied a red flag to the end of his lance and thrust it into the monster's cavern. Mistaking the cloth for meat, the dragon surged forward, 'rushing out of the cavern with his great mouth wide open'.

The Duke waited as the dragon bore down on him, great jaws agape, and drove itself onto the lance. 'The lance went right down its throat – down, down – and it died.' As is customary, the teller ends the tale by offering proof, averring that the monster's jawbone is, to this day, kept in a box in the sacristy of La Trinita: 'I have seen it myself – that's how I know that the story is true.'

Opposite: A Greek version of St George piercing the dragon's throat – a clear inspiration for the Dragon of La Trinita legend.

Chapter V

Thunderbirds of the Old West

~

Folklore does not reside solely in the past; it is an ongoing process of constant evolution and reinvention, so that folk tales – even dragon fables – can be found in any culture from any period. For example, American newspapers of the nineteenth and early twentieth centuries offer a rich crop of folk and tall tales, including now-celebrated accounts of a dragon-like cryptid that modern enthusiasts call the thunderbird.

In the Cleveland *Plain Dealer* of 22 April 1882, a report tells of how Thomas Campbell and Joseph Howard, two wood-choppers in California, had heard flapping overhead. 'We perceived . . . not more than 12 metres [forty feet] above the tree-tops, a creature that looked something like a crocodile . . . not less than 5 metres [18 feet] in length.' This extraordinary beast sported no less than six wings and twelve feet. They shot at it and although it 'uttered a cry similar to that of a calf and bear combined', it seemed to have an armoured hide and flew on.

A similar report from the *Tombstone Epitaph* of 26 April 1890, was headlined 'A Strange Winged Monster Discovered and Killed on the Huachuca Desert'.

Dragons of Fable and Folklore

Above: Late-19th-century Native American pictogram of a thunderbird, a legendary beast reported in some tall tales as closely resembling a dragon.

It told of 'a winged monster, resembling a huge alligator with . . . an immense pair of wings', spied by two ranchers over the desert. In a curious echo of the tired dragons of Thomas of Cantimpré (see page 88), 'the creature was evidently greatly exhausted by a long flight', and the men were able to bring it down with their Winchester rifles. Supposedly it was 28 metres (92 feet) long with a wingspan of 49 metres (160 feet)!

Iconography of the Dragon

Although the dragon has been an archetype of monstrous evil, especially in the Western, Christian tradition, it has also become an icon of ferocity, strength and domination, winning for itself a special place in the iconography of battle standards, coats of arms, flags and other symbols adopted by the powerful. This practice dates back to the earliest civilisations: the ancient mythical hero Marduk of Babylon had a dragon as his emblem.

Imperial windsock
The origins of the dragon as heraldic emblem in the Western tradition lie in the Roman army's adoption of the dragon as a military standard, meaning flag or banner, in the second century CE, a practice they borrowed from their foes the Sarmatians (an ancient Iranian people). Sarmatian cavalry bore metal dragon heads attached to wind-sock-like fabric, probably to show wind direction as an aid for equestrian archers. The Romans adapted the practice, and it is possible their version of the standard, known as a draco, and carried by a draconarius, was designed to generate a fearsome whistle/roar as wind passed through it and the fabric trailed out behind. Dragon standards and their bearers gained high status; the fourth-century Roman emperor Julian, for instance, was famously driven to fury when one of his draco standards was taken by the enemy.

Above: The Red Dragon of Wales, one of the Royal Beasts of sovereign iconography, which features on the coat of arms of the British monarchy.

Roman cavalry draco standards spread through the empire, making a particular impact in Britain. Post-Roman British rulers adopted the iconography of the dragon to add a touch of imperial glamour, giving rise to the legend of Vortigern, a Welsh king advised by the wizard Merlin, who uncovered battling red and white dragons. The red dragon was victorious, and was thereafter adopted as the 'red dragon dreadful' of Wales (*y Ddraig Goch*).

The terrible standard

A golden dragon was adopted by the Anglo-Saxons of Wessex, and a dragon standard is depicted in the Bayeux Tapestry. The dragon standard was taken up by the Normans, and used by many English kings thereafter. When Richard the Lionheart went on crusade (1191), he bore 'the terrible standard of the dragon in front unfurled', while at the Battle of Crecy (1346), King Edward III raised his 'unconquered standard of the Dragon Gules [i.e., red]'. Henry V bore a dragon standard at Agincourt (1415). Henry Tudor, who became Henry VII, made the Welsh red dragon a permanent feature of the English royal coat of arms, and dragon iconography was embraced enthusiastically by Henry VIII.

In heraldry, dragons have become a standard feature. The most common type is the four-footed version known to the Germans as a Lindwurm, which can be shown statant (all four feet on the ground), rampant (both forelegs raised), passant (one foreleg raised) or couchant (lying down). Another common variant is the two-legged version known as a wyvern, shown with a coiled tail.

Go dragons!

In the modern world the iconography of the dragon has been embraced above all by sports teams across

Above: Illustration of a 16th-century French knight in lavish livery, including a striking dragon helm.

the world, attracted by connotations of power and ferocity. Notable professional teams include the rugby league teams Catalan Dragons and St George Illawarra Dragons, the Welsh rugby union team Dragons RFC and the Japanese baseball team the Chunichi Dragons.

Chapter VI

Literary Dragons

From Romantic Epics
to Children's Fantasies

Chapter VI

Untangling literature from oral tradition, and literary fiction from other forms of writing, is a difficult undertaking. The dragons of Greek myth or Beowulf, of Japanese or German folklore, of Biblical visions or Mesopotamian epic, have come down to us through their written forms; arguably they are literary dragons. But if we take literature to signify those works written and disseminated to be read as art and/or entertainment, then literary dragons must wait for the emergence of a literary tradition.

One of the earliest and greatest literary fictions is the Chinese epic *Journey to the West*, compiled in the sixteenth century from earlier tales and traditions. It features traditional Chinese dragon kings and princes, but more specifically it develops one into a character in the novel, the shapeshifting White Dragon Horse. Similarly a traditional folkloric dragon is featured in an early work of Italian literature, Giambattista Basile's seventeenth-century collection of literary fairy tales, *Pentamerone* (in the tale, 'Lo Dragone'). Our modern literary tradition of dragons, however, which reached its apotheosis with Tolkien's dragon Smaug, owes more to the medieval romance tradition, the forerunner of the fantasy genre. Romances such as the *Alexander Romance*, a fantastical version of the life of Alexander the Great, or the Arthurian and Grail romances, which detailed the exploits of the legendary king and his knights, feature dragons in guises from transmogrified sorcerers to archetypal cave-dwelling monsters.

Literary Dragons

Above: Illumination from a 15th-century Alexander romance, showing the legendary king battling dragons with gems in their foreheads, also known as draconites (see page 92).

Chapter VI

Sired by a Dragon

∽

One of the earliest works of literature in the post-Classical Western canon was the *Alexander Romance*, a collection of tales about the life and deeds of Alexander the Great, which was popular in the courts of medieval Europe. Dragons feature at several points in the narrative. In one episode, Alexander's mother, Queen Olympias, is visited in her bed by the Egyptian pharaoh and sorcerer Nectanebo, in the guise of a dragon, which she believes to be an avatar of the god Ammon. Perhaps as a result of this unconventional parentage, Alexander is said to have had teeth as sharp as a serpent's. As an adult, he has a prophetic dream in which Ammon tells him: 'thou wilt encircle the whole world like a dragon'. Alexander actually encounters a dragon when founding the city of Alexandria; a local spirit, the Agathos Daimon, in the shape of a serpent-dragon, bothers his workmen, and he orders it slain, but then decrees it should be honoured with a shrine.

Arthur and his court were the subject of a whole cycle of medieval romance literature, but it is surprisingly light on dragons. The tale of one of Arthur's forebears, Vortigern, and his warring dragons

Above: Yvain and his leonine sidekick take on a wyvern, in an illustration from the 14th-century *Roman de Lancelot*.

(see page 113), was the most prominent, while Lancelot has a brief encounter with a dragon in the 'Prose Lancelot' (see pages 6–7). Dragons also feature in more obscure romances such as *Segurant, the Knight of the Dragon*, and *Yvain, the Knight of the Lion*, in which the eponymous hero rescues a lion from a dragon and the two become fast friends.

Chapter VI

Spenser's Dragons of Faerie

∽

A landmark in dragon literature, Edmund Spenser's epic late-sixteenth-century poem, *The Faerie Queene*, features the longest dragon battles in pre-modern literature. The six-volume poem relates both to Tudor and specifically Elizabethan monarchy, and to the triumph of Protestantism over Roman Catholicism. Dragons feature as allegories of evil.

In the first book, the virtuous Redcrosse Knight and his lady Una adventure through Fairyland, and encounter two monstrous dragons. The first, Errour, 'Halfe like a serpent horribly displaide, But th'other halfe did womans shape retaine'. Errour envelops Redcrosse in loathsome coils and vomits at him.

Redcrosse cuts off her head, but then has to face an even more terrible dragon, representing Satan himself, 'his body monstrous, horrible and vaste', swollen with 'wrath and poyson, and with bloody gore'. They battle for three days, during which Redcrosse has to be healed with sacred balms and even brought back to life, before finally thrusting his sword into the dragon's open jaw and bringing him crashing down so violently 'that th'earth him underneath did grone'.

Literary Dragons

Above: Woodcut from the 1598 3rd edition of Spenser's *The Faerie Queene*, showing the Redcrosse Knight battling a Satanic dragon, in a composition familiar from the tradition of images of St George.

Chapter VI

Above: John Tenniel's 1872 illustration for *Alice's Adventures in Wonderland* imagines the Jabberwocky as a dragon-like monster (although the poem itself makes no such claims).

Kids' Stuff?

Despite Spenser's vivid and dramatic portrayal of the dragon as the ultimate foe, serpent-monsters are striking by their relative absence from the Western literary tradition until late in the nineteenth century.

When they did reappear, it was in the burgeoning genre of children's fiction, and in a rather different guise. British writer Kenneth Grahame's 1898 short story 'The Reluctant Dragon' redefined the role of the dragon in fiction. In this fable the dragon looks fierce but is actually placid, lazy and inclined to poetry; makes friends with a young lad; and agrees to a mock battle to satisfy the bloodthirsty villagers. Children's writer Edith Nesbit compiled a whole book of dragon stories. Her well-known tale 'The Last of the Dragons' features a dragon who refuses to eat a princess and instead befriends her.

So began a rich tradition of dragons in children's literature, in which the scaly beast is a friend and ally. Notable examples include Cressida Cowell's *How To Train Your Dragon* series, the dragon of the Disney film *Pete's Dragon* (1977 and 2016) and the dragons of J. K. Rowling's *Harry Potter*, although these revert to type as a fearsome predators.

Chapter VI

Tolkien's Smaug

~

Smaug is probably the most famous dragon in history, let alone literature, 'A vast red-golden dragon . . . with wings folded like an immeasurable bat.' Created by John Ronald Reuel Tolkien, a professor of Anglo-Saxon at Oxford University, in his 1937 novel *The Hobbit*, Smaug is a composite of his literary forebears, most notably Fafnir and the unnamed dragon of Beowulf.

As the great exponent for the significance of the poem Beowulf, Tolkien appreciated as no other the mythic force of the dragon, and dragons populated his tales long before he started writing *The Hobbit*, in the early 1930s. For instance, his earlier work, *Farmer Giles of Ham*, a comic homage to medieval dragon fables, features a dragon called Chrysophylax.

Smaug – a name Tolkien said was derived from an Old English word, *sméogan*, meaning to creep through a hole – is a dragon who has invaded the halls of a dwarf-delved kingdom inside a mountain, and who jealously guards a giant pile of treasure. Just as in Beowulf, the theft of a single item arouses him from slumber, whereupon, like Fafnir, he engages in a battle of wits with his foe. Eventually Smaug issues

Above: Smaug stars in the 2014 Peter Jackson epic, *The Hobbit: The Battle of the Five Armies*.

forth to visit ruin on a nearby town, but is undone when a talking bird informs a heroic archer of the weak spot in the dragon's invulnerable armour. Combining a sharply drawn character study with the mythic power of his progenitors, Tolkien's Smaug is a memorable creation. Just as Tolkien's work has become definitive of the genre of high fantasy, despite not having invented it, so Smaug has become the definitive dragon of the modern imagination.

Modern Fantasy Literature

~

Fantasy as a genre was transformed by the popularity of Tolkien's *Lord of the Rings* in the 1960s. The most notable fantasy writer to come after Tolkien was Ursula K. Le Guin, whose *Earthsea* trilogy (1968–72) featured dragons and wizards in a recognisably Tolkienesque setting. The dragons of Earthsea are akin to Chinese *long*: remote, powerful, potentially dangerous, with little interest in human affairs. Their speech is magical and spellbinding. In 1968 Anne McCaffery published *Dragonflight*, the first in the *Dragonriders of Pern* series, in which dragons are aliens in the far future that can form psychic bonds with their riders, and jump through space and time.

In modern fantasy the best known dragons are those of George R. R. Martin. In *A Song of Ice and Fire* (1996), on which the series *Game of Thrones* is based (see page 152) dragons help their masters to become unstoppable conquerors while wreaking terrible destruction.

Opposite: An image from the *How to Train Your Dragon* film series, based on the best-selling books by Cressida Cowell.

Overleaf: A classic fantasy image pitting medieval knights against a fire-breathing dragon.

The Impossible Dragon

On the basis of ancient authorities, the writers of medieval bestiaries assumed that dragons were real creatures living in far away habitats. Even today, some people contend that historical depictions of dragons are evidence for the survival of dinosaurs into ancient times. An understanding of some simple principles of biology and physics shows, however, that dragons could never exist, at least not in the classical form of the winged, flying giant lizard.

The bigger they come
Constraints that mitigate against the reality of the dragon include body size, weight limits for flight and reptilian metabolism. For terrestrial animals, the main constraint on body size is that volume increases as the cube of length – a dragon ten times longer than, say, a monitor lizard, would have a volume (and thus mass) one thousand times greater. But the cross-sectional area of its bones would only be one hundred times greater, and therefore would not be able to support its weight.

This principle was memorably laid out in the 1928 essay 'On Being the Right Size', by the English philosopher and physiologist J. B. S. Haldane. He took the example of fictional giants, explaining that the giants 'would have broken their thighs every time they took a step. This is doubtless why they were sitting down in the picture I remember.'

Above: A 1663 etching by Wenceslaus Hollar, placing a wyvern-style dragon amidst an array of other exotic creatures.

The obvious objection to this logic is the evidence for titanic dinosaurs. These monstrous beasts, however, were only viable because they evolved truly massive leg bones and traded away speed and agility for their size. Even then, some palaeontologists have hypothesised certain extra factors, such as amphibious lifestyles, that made their immensity supportable.

Titanosaurs and sauropods are very far away from the image of the classical dragon, which is serpentine, lithe and agile. Modern reptiles are also limited by their metabolism, for they are cold-blooded. Unless dragons are conceived to be warm-blooded (as many dinosaurs probably were, along with their descendants, birds), it is hard to see how they could thrive and be active outside of the tropics, let alone in frigid northern lakes and caverns.

It'll never get off the ground

The mass principles constraining dragon size are especially relevant when the question of wings and flying is considered. The heaviest extant flying creature is probably the great bustard, which tips the scales at up to 20 kilograms (44 pounds), generally thought to be close to the mass limit for muscle-powered flight. Like all birds, it can only fly because of a raft of evolutionary adaptations such as lightweight honeycomb bone design.

Extinct animals such as the teratorn or the *Quetzalcoatlus* were even larger, and could reach wingspans of up to 10 metres (33 feet) and body mass up to 260 kilograms (570 pounds), but the classical dragon of folklore would have been much bigger than this. In order to fly, a creature weighing a ton or more might run into a paradox, for it would need to have flight muscles that weighed more than it did. It is also notable that the dragon of popular imagination has four legs and two wings, giving it a six-limbed body plan not found in any vertebrate.

Intriguingly though, the dragons being slaughtered by medieval saints are often much smaller than one would expect. And besides, some scientists have argued, albeit wrongly, that according to the laws of physics, even bumblebees should not be capable of getting off the ground.

Opposite: Illustrations from an encyclopedia by 17th-century-naturalist John Jonston, showing supposed species of dragon.

Tab. XII.

Draco bipes apteros captus in
Agro Bononiensi.

Draco alatus Apes
ex Grevino Aldro.

Figura ex Pareo.

Draco Æthiopicus.

Chapter VII

~

Dragon Hunting

~

How to Find
Your Dragon

Chapter VII

Dragons may not exist in the real world, but that does not mean they cannot be tracked down. The astute dragon hunter can gaze with awe upon some extraordinary examples, if they know where to look. This chapter introduces some of the most fruitful hunting grounds for the many excellent specimens to be discovered in the visual arts.

Artists have been depicting dragons for a long time. We saw in Chapter 1 how dragons featured in some of the oldest art in history, but it is likely that prehistoric cultures were drawing and carving dragons even before history began. A celebrated piece of dragon art from La Belle France cave in South Africa, known as the Horned Serpent, is only around two hundred years old, but was painted by the Later Stone Age San people, and may well reflect the kind of art made by Old Stone Age peoples of earlier eras. (Intriguingly the Horned Serpent cave painting also feeds into the debate about dinosaurs as inspiration for dragons, since it has been suggested that the dragon in the painting was modelled on fossils of dicynodont, a Permian-era therapsid.)

So, if you want to see a dragon for yourself, head to one of the museums, libraries, collections, galleries, palaces or churches mentioned in the following pages, where you may see anything from a Leonardo da Vinci cartoon dragon to a Japanese wall hanging.

Opposite: Dragons were popular in Japan's *ukiyo-e* woodblock print tradition, as in this 19th-century example by Utagawa Kuniyoshi.

Chapter VII

The Ishtar Gate

~

Visitors to ancient Babylon in the era of Nebuchadnezzar were treated to dazzling sights, starting with the monumental Ishtar Gate. A high arch spanned the gap between two mighty towers decorated with brightly coloured enamelled bricks and reliefs of fearsome dragons and bulls. An inscription in the voice of Nebuchadnezzar proclaims: 'I placed wild bulls and ferocious dragons in the gateways and thus adorned them with luxurious splendour so that people might gaze on them in wonder.'

Today these intriguing *mušḫuššu* dragons inhabit a reconstructed part of the gate in Berlin's Pergamon Museum. With the head and scales of a snake, claws of an eagle, legs of a lion, scorpion-like tail and prominent horn, they have prompted speculation they are based on a real creature. Robert Koldewey, the archaeologist who excavated the Ishtar Gate in the early twentieth century, believed the dragons could have been based on iguanadon fossils. Belgian cryptozoologist Bernard Heuvelmans linked the Ishtar dragon to the mokele-mbembe of central Africa, another suspected prehistoric survivor. Another possibility might be the Sivatherium, an extinct giraffid with a long neck and horns on its head.

Dragon Hunting

Above: Detail of one of the celebrated *mušuššu* dragons of the Ishtar Gate. Note the hybrid features.

Chapter VII

Above: Detail of a dragon from the Ming Dynasty Datong Nine Dragon Wall.

The Nine Dragon Walls

There are three notable Nine Dragon Walls (or Screens) in China, as well as replicas in other places (e.g., Canada). They are large screen walls decorated with enormous friezes of colourful glazed ceramics, depicting nine ornate, writhing dragons, each playing with a pearl. Two of the walls are in Beijing, in Beihei Park (the smallest and most delicate) and in front of Taiji Gate of the Forbidden City, where a wall 20.4 metres (67 feet) long and 3.5 metres (11½ feet) high is decorated with 270 pieces of glaze.

The largest and oldest of the walls is in Datong, in Shanxi Province. Constructed during the Ming Dynasty (1271–1368), the wall is 45.5 metres (150 feet) long and 8 metres (26 feet) high. The dragons are depicted in yellow, blue, purple and white, backed by a landscape of mountains, rivers and trees. Below the main frieze is a plinth decorated with forty-one images of two dragons playing with a pearl (a kind of mating dance between male and female dragons), and depictions of other fauna. The Nine Dragon Walls are virtuoso demonstrations of artistic skill and craftsmanship, intended to impress imperial subjects and celebrate a creature that was traditionally associated with the Chinese imperial throne.

Chapter VII

Illuminated Manuscripts

∾

Before the printing press, wealthy institutions and patrons in medieval Europe would commission highly skilled craftsmen and artists to copy out, illustrate and decorate works onto vellum (treated animal skin); these are known as illuminated manuscripts. Illustrations focused on initial letters as well as breaking up the text; often beautiful and artistic, they could also be quirky, comical, gruesome and strange.

This is especially true of the dragons in illuminated manuscripts, which include some of the most striking and downright peculiar representations. Most commonly they are being conquered by a variety of saints and representing evil in general and Satan in particular.

The attributes of such dragons varied wildly, from zoologically plausible lizard or crocodile-like beasts, like the web-toed dragon subdued by St George in a late-fifteenth-century Dutch Huth Hours; to fanciful, such as the two-headed, eight-legged, crowned dragons with eye-covered torsos, shown assailing Alexander in a fifteenth-century French *True History of Good King Alexander*. A fourteenth-century French *Apocalypse* manuscript shows a wyvern-like beast from

Above: St Margaret bursts forth from the belly of the beast in this illumination from a 15th-century Dutch Book of Hours.

the end of days, while in Joachim de Fiore's *Vaticinia de Pontificibus*, a fifteenth-century Italian manuscript, the contested papacy of Urban VI is represented as a bizarre human-headed, horned satanic dragon, sporting a fetching cardinal's hat.

Chapter VII

Dragon Relics

∼

In Early Modern Europe faith in the reality of dragons was still very much up for grabs, and those inclined to believe could point to tangible proof in the form of specimens displayed in multiple institutions. These were put on show in line with the tradition of *Wunderkammer* ('cabinets of curiosities'), in which marvels of nature were collected to illustrate the wonder of creation. Some of these can still be seen in museums today.

Many of them were old bones – particularly of prehistoric creatures – especially those collected from caves where dragons were thought likely to live. Johannes Hain's 1672 *Of the Dragons of the Carpathian Caverns* includes drawings of cave-bear bones discovered in caves in the Carpathians, known today as Drachenhöhle and Drachenlock Cave. Such bones can now be seen in churches including Wawel Cathedral in Kraków, Murano's Church of Santa Maria e San Donato and the Cathedral of San Leucio in Atessa.

More impressively, whole dragon specimens could be viewed (for a fee) in private cabinets, such as Ulisse Aldrovandi's late-sixteenth-century museum in Bologna, or the amazing Hydra of Hamburg. When

Dragon Hunting

Above: A copy of a 1734 illustration of the notorious Hydra of Hamburg, by the Dutch naturalist Albert Seba, who believed the creature to be genuine.

Swedish naturalist Carl Linnaeus visited Hamburg in 1735 he revealed the Hydra to be a fake, made from snakeskin and weasel, but his public debunking upset the monster's owners and he left town under a cloud. A surviving stuffed dragon that can still be seen today is the Brněnský drak (Dragon of Brno), which hangs in a passageway in the Czech city, but disappointingly is obviously a crocodile.

Chapter VII

Art Dragons

With their strange and terrible form, and dramatic habits, dragons have obvious attraction as a subject for figurative artists, but even abstract artists have found inspiration from the king of monsters. Dragons featured in masterpieces from China, such as Chen Rong's 1244 painted handscroll 'Nine Dragons'. For European painters, battles between saints and dragons were a popular subject – obvious examples include Gentileschi, Raphael and Ucello. Perhaps the biggest dragon fan of the Renaissance was Leonardo da Vinci, whose notebooks display a dazzling array of the creatures, as well as instructions for how to draw them: 'take for its head that of a hound, with the eyes of a cat, the ears of a porcupine, the nose of a greyhound, the brow of a lion.'

Dragon-like forms haunt the work of Albrecht Dürer (*Heaven and Hell*, 1471) and William Blake (*The Great Red Dragon* paintings, 1805–10). By the nineteenth century, dragons akin to the modern conception emerge in art; the ceta of Frederick Lord Leighton's *Perseus and Andromeda*, or the wyrm of Arthur Rackham's *St George and the Dragon* would not look out of place in a modern movie. More recently, surrealists such as Leonora Carrington and Dorothea Tanning embraced the iconography of

Dragon Hunting

Above: William Blake's *The Great Red Dragon* (*c.*1804), part of a series inspired by verses from the Book of Revelation.

the dragon, as in Carrington's 1979 tapestry, *Dragon*, while in Kenyan American artist Wangechi Mutu's 2007 collage *A Dragon Kiss Always Ends in Ashes*, the monster becomes an agent of gender-based violence.

Modern Dragons

Always popular, dragons have conquered the world in recent decades, as both a cause and consequence of the ever-increasing popularity of fantasy in culture and media. The roots of the modern dragon craze can be traced back to the flowering of fantasy literature that bloomed in the wake of Tolkien's success (see page 126), although this itself was a slow-burning phenomenon. Tolkien's magnum opus *The Lord of the Rings* (LOTR) was published in three volumes between 1954 and 1955, but did not become a smash hit until the mid-1960s. Smaug's popularity predated that of LOTR, since *The Hobbit* had been a success from its publication in 1937.

Dungeons & Dragons
The growing popularity of fantasy literature in the 1960s spawned other fantasy media, notably the role-playing game *Dungeons & Dragons*, a.k.a. D&D, first published in 1974. In D&D players use their imagination to play as characters in a Tolkienesque setting, battling monsters drawn from the canon of world myth, folklore and fiction. Dragons, as the game's title suggests, are pre-eminent amongst them, varying from godlike beings based on the ancient Mesopotamian Tiamat to wyverns out of heraldry. The primary template, however, is Smaug, and by extension the tradition of Beowulf and Fafnir to which he is heir. The art of D&D and related

Above: Dinosaur-like dragon monster created by Ray Harryhausen, from the 1958 film *The 7th Voyage of Sinbad*.

publications, alongside the cover art of fantasy literature, played an important role in defining, expanding and spreading the modern visual identity of dragons.

Monster movies

Role-playing games like D&D went through waves of popularity, until the success of the *Lord of the Rings* movie trilogy (2001–3) catapulted fantasy into the mainstream of global culture. Although they didn't actually feature any dragons (unless one counts the dragon-adjacent Fell Beasts), the movies either revealed or created a popular hunger for the tropes of fantasy in mass media. Dragons had been on the screen before, from the cuddly one in *Pete's Dragon* (1977) to the more classic fantasy of *Dragonheart* (1996), which loosely mimics the plot of Kenneth Grahame's story 'The Reluctant Dragon' (see page 125). Now, however, they would achieve a much higher profile in works such as the animated franchise *How to Train Your Dragon* (the first movie of which was released in 2010) and the television phenomenon *Game of Thrones* (2011–19). The success of the latter, alongside the cinematic incarnation of Smaug in *The Hobbit: The Desolation of Smaug* (2012), pushed dragons to new heights of popularity.

Dragon world
In the atomised universe of modern media, dragons inhabit a huge variety of niches, from mainstream TV franchises and movies; comic books, manga and anime; computer, board, card, desktop and role-playing games; and fringe internet culture. To give just one example, the Japanese media franchise *Dragon Ball*, based loosely on the Chinese epic *Journey to the West*, and concerning a quest to summon various dragons, has spawned multiple animated series and no less than twenty-one animated feature films, while the original manga series

Above: James Cameron's 2009 blockbuster movie *Avatar* featured flying aliens clearly modelled on dragons.

Overleaf: One of the dragons from *Game of Thrones*, tipping the balance of power on the battlefield.

has sold more than 260 million copies worldwide. There are now communities of people fantasising, writing, messaging, cosplaying and role-playing as dragons, including so-called dragonkin – people who identify as dragons, or even believe that they are dragons in human bodies, and dress, act and even modify their bodies accordingly.

Further Reading

Books

A Dictionary of Fairies: Hobgoblins, Brownies, Bogies and Other Supernatural Creatures, Katharine Briggs, Penguin, 1993

A Little History of Dragons, Joyce Hargreaves, Wooden Books, 2006

A Natural History of the Unnatural World, Joel Levy, Carroll & Brown Publishers, 2000

A Song of Fire and Ice, George R. R. Martin, HarperCollins, 2012

Beowulf: A New Verse Translation, Seamus Heaney, Faber and Faber, 1999

Chinese Myths and Folk Tales, Barnes & Noble, 2020

D&D Monster Manual, Wizards of the Coast, 5th revised edition, 2014

Dictionary of Asian Mythology, David Adams Leeming, OUP, 2001

Earthsea: The First Four Books, Ursula LeGuin, Penguin, 2012

Myths from Mesopotamia Creation, The Flood, Gilgamesh, and Others, trans: Stephanie Dalley, Oxford World's Classics, 2008

Natural History, Pliny the Elder (Author), John Healey (Introduction, Translator), Penguin Classic, 1991

On Being the Right Size and Other Essays, J. B. S. Haldane (Author), John Maynard Smith (Editor), Oxford Paperbacks, 1985

The Book of Dragons, E. Nesbit, Read & Co., 2011

The Chinese Myths: A Guide to the Gods and Legends, Tao Tao Liu, Thames and Hudson, 2022

The Dragon in the West: From Ancient Myth to Modern Legend, Daniel Ogden, OUP, 2021

The Dragon: Fear and Power, Martin Arnold, Reaktion Books, 2018

The Faerie Queene, Edmund Spenser, Penguin Classics, 2003

The Greek Alexander Romance, Penguin Classics, Richard Stoneman, 1991

The Greek Myths: The Complete and Definitive Edition, Robert Graves, Penguin, 2017

The Hobbit, J. R. R. Tolkien, HarperCollins, 2000

The Lore of the Land, Jacqueline Simpson and Jennifer Westwood, Penguin, 2006

The Medieval Romance of Alexander: The Deeds and Conquests of Alexander the Great, Jehan Wauquelin (Author), Nigel Bryant (Translator), D. S. Brewer, 2019

The Nibelunglied, trans: A. Hatto, Penguin Classics, 2024

The Penguin Book of Classical Myths Paperback, Jennifer March, Penguin, 2009

The Penguin Book of Dragons, Scott G. Bruce (Editor), Penguin Classics (2022)

The Rig Veda, [trans] Wendy Doniger, Penguin Classics, 2005

The Saga of the Volsungs with The Saga of Ragnar Lothbrok, Jackson Crawford, Penguin Classics 2017

The Watkins Book of English Folktales, Neil Philip, Watkins, 2022

Online Resources

'Anatomy of a Dragon', British Library Medieval Manuscripts Blog, blogs.bl.uk/digitisedmanuscripts/2014/04/the-anatomy-of-a-dragon.html

'Database of Japanese Folklore', Yokai.com

'Draconika Dragons', draconika.com

'Dragons in Greek Mythology', theoi.com/greek-mythology/dragons.html

'Fifty British Dragon Tales: an Analysis', J. Simpson, Folklore, 1978, Vol. 89, No. 1, jstor.org/stable/1260098

'Finding Dragons in Early Modern Europe', Centre for Reformation and Early Modern Studies, more.bham.ac.uk/crems/2023/06/02/finding-dragons-in-early-modern-europe/

'Natural History of Dragons', American Museum of Natural History, amnh.org/exhibitions/mythic-creatures/dragons/natural-history-of-dragons

'The History of Dragons in Art', muddycolors.com/2022/10/the-history-of-dragons-in-art/

'The Medieval Bestiary', bestiary.ca

Index

Agathos Daimon 120
Aido Hwedo 51
Alexander the Great 90, 93, 144
   Alexander Romance 118–21
alligators 36–7, 111
art dragons 148–9
Arthurian legend 6, 120–1
attributes 90
   bad breath and long life 92
   draconites 92–3

Bagrada dragon 68, 70
Beowulf 8, 9, 54, 60, 67, 92, 118, 126, 150
bestiaries 76, 86–9, 132
Biblical dragons 9, 25, 65, 76, 87, 93

Cetus (*cetae*) 18, 29, 68
children's literature 125
Chinese dragons 118, 142–3
   Chinese *long* dragons 34–7
Chrysophylax 126
Church Fathers 76, 78–9
Cnoc na Cnoimh 65
Colchian dragon 14, 18
crocodiles 110, 144, 147

dinosaurs 133, 138
dragon festivals 44–5
Dragon King 41, 42, 71
dragon standards 112
   English kings 114
   imperial Rome 112–14
   sports teams 114–15

dragon world 152–3
dragons 6–9
   anatomical impossibility 132–3
   flight 134
Dungeons & Dragons 150–1

Errour 122

Fafnir 60–3, 68, 100, 126, 150
fossil bones 28–9, 36, 78, 146

Gonggong, the Black Dragon 41

habitats 68
   air-dwellers 71
   going underground 70
   wastelands 70–1
   water monsters 68–70
Hellmouth 79
heraldry 113, 114
Huanglong, the Yellow Dragon 49
Hydra 8, 18
   Hydra of Hamburg 146–7

illuminated manuscripts 144–5
Ishtar Gate 9, 140–1
Ismenian dragon 18–19

Japanese dragons 42–3, 138
Jörmungandr, Midgard Serpent 18, 55–7, 64, 68

La Trinita Dragon 109
La Velue 103
Labbu 16

Ladon 18
Lambton Worm 100–1, 105
Le Guin, Ursula K. 129
Leviathan 25
Lindwurm 114
  Lindwurm of Klagenfurt 29
Linnaeus, Carl 147
Linton Worm 65

Martin, George R. R. 129
McCaffery, Anne 129
Mester Stoorworm 64–5
movies 151–3

Ninazu 16
Nine Dragon Walls 142–3
Ninki Nanka 51

Peluda 90, 103
Python 18

Quetzalcóatl 49

Rainbow Serpent 51
Red Dragon of Wales 113–14
reptiles 30, 132–3
Roman dragons 26–7
Ryūjin 42

saints and dragons 81–3, 92
serpent-dragons 14, 16–17,
  18–19, 22–3, 25, 42, 51, 57,
  83, 90, 120
seven-headed dragon of the
  Apocalypse 9, 76, 93
Sigurd 8, 9, 60–3, 100

Smaug 63, 118, 126–7, 150, 152
Spenser, Edmund *The Faerie
  Queene* 122–3
St George's dragon 70–1,
  80–3, 98, 109, 144
Stone Age dragons 138

Taniwha 51
Tarasque 102–3
Thomas of Cantimpré
  88–9, 111
thunderbirds 49–51, 110–11
Tiamat 8, 16, 22, 25, 36, 68
Tolkien, J. R. R. 6, 54, 126–7,
  129, 150

Vinci, Leonardo da 9, 138, 148–9
Vortigern 99, 113–14, 120–1
Vritra 8–9, 22–3, 57, 68

Wantley Dragon 104–5
wyrms 8–9, 54, 100
wyverns 114, 121, 133,
  144–5, 150

Picture Credits

The publisher would like to thank the following for permission to reproduce copyright material:

Gift of Mrs. Richard E. Danielson and Mrs. Chauncey McCormick, The Art Institute of Chicago 4; /Photo © Photo Josse/Bridgeman Images 7; /Bridgeman Images 11; /Bequest of Phyllis Massar, 2011, Metropolitan Museum of Art 15; /Pictures from History/Bridgeman Images 17; /Daderot via Wikimedia 19 Photo © Fine Art Images/Bridgeman Images; / Sailko via Wikimedia 23; /Gustavé Dore 24; /From the British Library archive/Bridgeman Images 27; /Fondo Antiguo de la Biblioteca de la Universidad de Sevilla via Wikimedia 29; / Biodiversity Library via Wikimedia 31; /Fletcher Fund, 1936 via The Met 35; /Michele and Tom Grimm/Alamy Stock Photo 37; /Gift of Charles Lang Freer, National Museum of Asian Art, Smithsonian 38-39; /British Museum via Wikimedia 40; /Pictures from History/Bridgeman Images 43; /The New York Public Library 45; /Karen Su/China Span/Alamy Stock Photo 46-47; /Burfalcy via Wikimedia 49; /PHAS/Universal Images Group via Getty Images 50; / Arni Magnusson Institute/Bridgeman Images 55; /Royal Academy of Arts,The Yorck Project (2002) via Wikimedia 57; /Fra Dansk Skolemuseum, AU Library, Campus Emdrup via Wikimedia Commons; /The Stapleton Collection/Bridgeman Images 61; /Werner Forman/Universal Images Group/Getty Images 62; /Michael Maggs via Wikimedia 65; /Public domain 66, 69; / Niday Picture Library/Alamy Stock Photo 72-73; /Rogers Fund, 1912, The Met 77; /From the British Library archive/Bridgeman Images 79; /Universal History Archive/UIG /Bridgeman Images 80; /Art Images via Getty Images 83; /Public Domain 84-85; /The J. Paul Getty Museum, Los Angeles, Ms. 100, fol. 54, 2007.16.54 86; /Public domain 89; /Classic Image/ Alamy Stock Photo 91; /Gameover/Alamy Stock Photo 93; /Bridgeman Images 94-95; / Lambeth Palace Library/Bridgeman Images 99; /From the British Library archive/Bridgeman Images 101; /Stefano Bianchetti/Bridgeman Images 103; /Science History Images/Alamy Stock Photo 105; /Charles Walker Collection/Alamy Stock Photo 106-107; /Religious Stock/ Alamy Stock Photo 108; /Look and Learn/Elgar Collection/Bridgeman Images 111; /Universal History Archive/UIG /Bridgeman Images 113; /Florilegius/Universal Images Group via Getty Images 115; /Pictures from History/Bridgeman Images 119; /Archives Charmet/Bridgeman Images 121; /Granger/Bridgeman Images 123; /Chronicle/Alamy Stock Photo 124; /Warner Bros Entertainment Inc./Everett Collection/Bridgeman Images 127; /Landmark Media/ Alamy Stock Photo 128; /© Gino D'Achille. All rights reserved 2025/Bridgeman Images 130-131; /Hollar, W., Animalium, Ferarum, & Bestiarum (1663) 133; /Biodiversity Heritage Library 135; /Pictures from History/Bridgeman Images 139; /Osama Shukir Muhammaed Amin FRCP (Glasg) 141; /Lao Mao/Shutterstock 142; /From the British Library archive/Bridgeman Images 145; /Paul D Stewart/Science Photo Library 149; /Everett Collection/Bridgeman Images 151; / Album/Alamy Stock Photo 153, 154-155

Every effort has been made to acknowledge correctly and contact the source and/or copyright holder of each picture and UniPress Books apologizes for any unintentional errors or omissions, which will be corrected in future editions of this publication.

Author Credits

With thanks to Jason Hook and Ruth Patrick at UniPress.